乌达木和他的马

WU DA MU
HE TA DE MA

张　慧
费西儿·米勒◎著

新　华　出　版　社

图书在版编目（CIP）数据

乌达木和他的马：汉英对照/张慧，费西儿·米勒著
北京：新华出版社，2015.4
ISBN 978－7－5166－1605－5
Ⅰ.①乌…　Ⅱ.①张…②费…　Ⅲ.①英语—儿童读物　Ⅳ.①H319.4
中国版本图书馆 CIP 数据核字（2015）第 069447 号

乌达木和他的马

作　　者：张　慧　费西儿·米勒

出 版 人：张百新　　**责任编辑**：贾允河
封面设计：伍民力

出版发行：新华出版社
地　　址：北京石景山区京原路 8 号
邮　　编：100040
网　　址：http：//www.xinhuapub.com
经　　销：新华书店
购书热线：010－63077122
中国新闻书店购书热线：010－63072012

照　　排：新华出版社照排中心
印　　刷：北京凯达印务有限公司

成品尺寸：150mm×230mm
印　　张：6.4　　**字　　数**：60 千字
版　　次：2015 年 11 月第一版
印　　次：2015 年 11 月第一次印刷

书　　号：ISBN 978－7－5166－1605－5
定　　价：16.00 元

内容简介

午夜，乌达木做了一个梦。梦中，他和一匹英俊的白马迷失在草原上，一起度过了一段愉快的时光。梦醒时分，让他更加珍惜他和干妈、干爸之间的那份真情。全文意境优美，充满诗情画意。笔触勾画出一幅草原上大自然的真善美童话境界。

About the story : One night, Uudam had a dream. In his dream, he, in pajamas, got lost on a foggy immense grassland in Inner Mongolia, China. He happened to meet a handsome white horse on the grassland. Then they spent some time together, and had a lot of fun. When he woke up from his dream, he appreciates more the love and support from his Godparents. It is kind of a fairy tale and very poetic and touches readers' hearts deeply.

午夜，乌达木做了一个梦。

梦里，乌达木身着睡衣，在大草原上迷失了。周围都是雾，什么都看不见。

“乌达木——”、“乌达木——”有人喊他。

乌达木转过身，看到一匹英俊的白马从雾中向他走来。乌达木愣愣地看着白马。

白马蹲下，乌达木翻身上马。

乌达木：这是哪里？我们去哪儿？

白马：你不是有 GPS 吗？

乌达木：我没有带 GPS。

白马：那就看北斗星吧。我们先四处走走，只要能在一年后的今日子时回到这里，我就可以把你送回家。

乌达木：你这是什么意思？

白马：我好孤独。你就放下学习，陪我一会儿吧！

乌达木：好吧。

前方出现一个敖包。

乌达木：请在敖包处停下。

白马：我们时间不多，你要快点。

在敖包处，乌达木下马，跪下磕头。

乌达木：如果真有天堂，愿阿爸和额吉在天堂相见相伴。儿子乌达木多么想有你们的陪伴。乌达木好想你们！

乌达木起身，从左向右绕三圈。

乌达木上马，他们继续前进。

沉默了一会儿。

白马：你愿意回到从前吗？

乌达木：如果能。

白马：但时光不会倒流。

乌达木：时光可以在脑中倒流，可以在梦中倒流。

白马：现实中，时光是不会倒流的，只有继续往前走。这一切都是上帝的意志。

乌达木：愿上帝保佑！

白马：我渴了，什么时候可以喝到水？

乌达木：看到河就有水了。

白马：我也知道看到河就有水了。问题是河在哪里？

乌达木：我也渴。呼伦贝尔大草原上有 7 条河。请耐心一点。

乌达木：海拉尔金帐汗草原上有一条河，九曲十八弯，我们叫她莫日格勒河，是“天下第一曲水”。内蒙古和俄国边境有一条河叫额尔古纳河，还有……

白马：你在谈河解渴？

乌达木：我希望你充满希望。

夜晚，好黑暗。

乌达木：听，有河水在唱歌，那是莫日格勒河。

白马：天色太黑了，我没有看到河。

乌达木：河水的歌声不会逃过我的耳朵。往左边走。

白马：怎么还没有到？

乌达木：请耐心一点，朋友，前方就是。

白马：我看到河了。希望成真了。

乌达木：你喝水，我要生个篝火。

篝火照亮了河水，照亮了一片草原，照亮了乌达木的脸庞，照亮了白马的脸庞。

乌达木躺在篝火边的草地上，仰望天空。

白马：你为什么不去喝水？在想什么呢？

乌达木：想阿爸和额吉。他们给我生命，并看护我和姐姐。爸爸妈妈一起放羊，他们是快乐的牧羊人。他们又一起回到了天堂。他们是好爸爸好妈妈，我永远为他们感到骄傲。我好想他们，想同妈妈一起唱歌的那些时光，想同爸爸一起骑马的那些日子。他们永远活在我的心中。

白马：我也没有阿爸和额吉，我也一样坚强的生活下去。虽然是你在陪我，你不觉得是我在陪你吗？现在我的任务就是陪你。这就是我的“人生”。在人类面前，你要做一个男子汉。在我们蒙古族，男人的眼泪是珍珠，是不可以轻易流的。可在我面前，你可以不做男子汉吗？

乌达木：那做什么？

白马：做你自己。

乌达木：我想唱首歌。

白马：唱吧。

乌达木唱：

作词：特古斯吉日嘎拉
作曲：拉格巴苏荣
汉语填词：布仁巴雅尔

美丽的花朵不要摘下它
它不想离开大地的怀抱
亲爱的妈妈你牵着我的手
轻轻地讲过它的心愿
你在远方

我的母亲
梦中却总在牵着我的手

风沙弥漫遮住了双眼
我总想听见妈妈的呼唤
你在哪里
我的妈妈
好想让你轻轻地吻我
你在远方
我的母亲
梦中的你在亲吻着我的脸

唱到这里，乌达木已泣不成声，泪流满面。
过了一会儿，乌达木接着唱：

你要我勇敢像云中的雄鹰
你让我坚强像风中的花朵
当我昂起头大步向前走

我知道你会永远陪伴着我
你在远方
我的母亲
梦中的你在紧紧地拥抱着我

白马：你唱的是《梦中的额吉》。

乌达木：你怎么知道？

白马：全国人民都知道。马民们也知道。都知道你想你的额吉。

乌达木：是的，每时每刻。额吉教给我很多歌，这也是额吉教给我的歌。我唱这首歌是来怀念她。

白马：哭一下好受一点吗？

乌达木：好受一点。

白马：也想阿爸了吧？

乌达木：是。阿爸在世时的工作是帮雇主放羊，我会常常帮阿爸一起放羊。有一次写作业，一只小羊羔吃掉了我的作业本。

白马：这样啊？

乌达木：是的。

白马：你会学羊叫吗？

乌达木：当然会。

白马：模仿一下。

乌达木：咩——咩——咩——

乌达木：我还会学你叫呢。

白马：比如？

乌达木：你听！

白马：我听。

乌达木：你听！

白马：我听着呢。你怎么这么啰嗦。

乌达木：嘶——嘶——嘶——

白马：像！像！我怀疑你前生是马。

乌达木：你怎么不说我是羊？

白马：好！你是羊，我是人。

乌达木：你怎么不说你是羊？

白马：好！我是羊，你不是人。

乌达木：说话要文明。

白马：偶尔幽默一下也没什么不好么。其实，我不太会说话，我说你不是人，是想说你是雄鹰。你是蒙古草原上的雄鹰。其实我真真想说的是，你是个好孩子，你是你奶奶心目中的巴特尔，你也是我心目中的巴特尔。好了，想爸爸，就再唱首《献给父亲的歌》吧。

乌达木唱：

作词：敖特根森德

作曲：敖特根森德

汉语填词：布仁巴雅尔

秋风摇曳

草木发黄

我的父亲

在变苍老

山鹿健壮时节

我要前往故乡

不等流水换冰装

渴望叩见父亲

遥望山峰

想念父亲

河水清澈见底

像我父亲善良

山鹿健壮时节

我要前往故乡

不等流水换冰装

渴望叩见父亲

秋意绵绵

军龄催人

渴望快点见到

父亲泪满笑脸

山鹿健壮时节

我要前往故乡

不等流水换冰装

渴望叩见父亲

白马：你的歌唱得好感人，令我也开始想念我的爸爸和妈妈了。

乌达木：我的阿爸额吉是一级火箭，把我送到了接近星空的地方；我的干爸和干妈是二级火箭，接力把我送入了星空。我是一颗星，一颗闪亮的星，但代价太大：阿爸额吉付出了生命，干爸干妈也为此付出了很多很多。

白马：那是上帝的意志。你是为歌唱而生，你是我们蒙古族的骄傲。

停了一会儿，

白马：你长大后想当什么？

乌达木：我想当科学家。

白马：别忘了，你是为歌唱而生，继续唱歌不好吗？

乌达木：你认为蒙古族人会停止唱歌吗？

白马：我是说专业唱歌。

乌达木：干爸是中国国际广播电台的一名新闻工作者，同时也唱歌。我可以是科学家，同时也唱歌，只要大家还喜欢听我唱。

白马：你的歌声中有你发明的神奇的绿色墨水，有草原的清香，有奔流的河水，有千里马，有对亲人无限的思念，令人感动，令人重新审视对待大自然的态度和对待亲人的态度。我是你的粉丝。

乌达木：谢谢你，亲爱的粉丝！如果你不渴了，我们继续前进吧！

白马：是，草原小王子！

乌达木：我们比赛吧！我是学校的 1000 米冠军。

白马：那就来吧！谁怕谁啊？

乌达木和白马赛跑。

乌达木远远落后。

白马回头，跑过来，蹲下。

乌达木上马。

白马：你没有发现人类也有局限性吗？

乌达木：我从没说没有。不要哪壶不开提哪壶。

白马：我没有那个意思。只是想告诉你，人

类和马类或其它类，各有长处，相互尊重，相互学习，友好相处。

乌达木：你读过书吗？

白马：这是常识。书里的东西，不过是常识的书面表达。没有常识，哪里写得出书？

天亮了，雾散了。

白马：瞧，前面好多人，他们都在干什么？看，有一个人正在点燃火炬。

乌达木：一定是那达慕！

白马：那达慕是什么？

乌达木：那达慕大会是内蒙古族人民一年一

度的传统节日。

白马：点火炬的人是谁？

乌达木：是才德双全的巴特尔。

白马：巴特尔是什么意思？

乌达木：巴特尔是英雄的意思。你刚才还说我是你的巴特尔。

白马：我有说吗？

乌达木：你没说吗？

白马：我当然说了！

乌达木：你当然说了！

白马：他们在唱什么？

乌达木：你仔细听。

草原上，众人齐唱，歌声悠扬：

蔚蓝的天空飘着吉祥的白云，
碧绿的草原花儿五彩缤纷，
丰收时节草原的盛会，
聚集着成吉思汗的子孙。

牧民儿女跃马扬鞭纵横驰骋，
姑娘弓满如月箭穿靶心。
老额吉举着哈达为巴特尔祝福，
老阿爸抱着奶酒献给勇敢之神。

啊荷荷，开放时代出英雄，这才是草原上的蒙古人！

夜色的降临满天是闪烁的星辰，
熊熊燃烧的篝火是那么的温馨，
丰收时节草原的盛会，
各族朋友犹如一家亲。

酒酣高唱《美丽的草原我的家》，
入夜拉起《万马奔腾》马头琴。

啊荷荷，挽手跳起欢乐舞，让我们永远心连着心！

那达慕之歌选自《中国大百科全书·民族卷》

白马：那达慕一定有赛马，对吧？你参

加吗？

乌达木：你参加吗？

白马：你参加吗？

乌达木：亲爱的白马，你不要啰嗦，马赛就在那边。加速，跳进去，加入他们。

白马飞过人群，落在赛马场上的起跑线上。

令枪响后，他们跑在了中间，跑在了前面。

人群中的人们认出了乌达木。

“乌达木——”、“乌达木——”、“乌达木——”“加油！加油！”

乌达木和他亲爱的白马冲过终点线！

乌达木：我们赢了！谢谢你，亲爱的马！

白马：什么时候学会客气啦？

乌达木：不是客气，是真诚的！我们快走，否则大家围上来让我签字，我们就走不掉了。

白马：那边的人堆是干什么的？

乌达木：什么人堆？还马堆呢。

白马：如有冒犯，请原谅。

乌达木：你已经被原谅了。

白马：你还没有回答我的问题。

乌达木：什么问题？

白马：那边的人堆在干什么？不，不，那边

的人们在干什么？很多人的脖子上有彩旗飘扬。

乌达木：脖子上围有彩旗的人是摔跤手。

白马：你去摔跤吗？

乌达木：你去摔跤吗？

白马：摔跤与我有关系吗？

乌达木：凡事都试试嘛！

白马：要试，你试吧！

乌达木：我会的！

白马：赛马，我可以帮你；摔跤，我只有袖手旁观了。

乌达木：那你就袖手旁观吧！

乌达木往后退了几步，纵身一跃，跳进摔跤比赛场。

比赛开始，乌达木像雄鹰展翅，飞向对面的摔跤手。

对面的“雄鹰”迎面扑来。

然后，他们握手致意。

很快，乌达木被对方抱起，重重地摔倒在地。很快，那位“雄鹰”又把乌达木扶了起来。

裁判拉起获胜选手的手，高高举起，宣布胜利属于那位“雄鹰”。

乌达木伸手与那位胜利的雄鹰握手，然后离开。

白马同乌达木继续前进。

白马：你明明知道你摔不过他，你为什么还要去同他比试？

乌达木：为了吉祥三宝！

白马：为了你和你干爸，还有你干妈？

乌达木：为了另外一种吉祥三宝。摔跤比赛的意义在于，作为一个男子汉，你要让自己变得有力量。如果输了，说明你还不够有力量，你要多干活，多锻炼；体力上光有力量还不够，还要有意志，有风范。知道摔不过对方，也要去试一试，这是意志；输了就认输，并向赢者致敬，这是风范。体力，意志，风范也是吉祥三宝。其实，马赛不也是一样吗？体力加意志加风范，你也有吉祥三宝，不是吗？

白马：你这样看我吗？

乌达木：不是我这样看你，是我这样看马类。我从你们身上也学到很多东西。

白马：你这样说，我很高兴。

乌达木：我很高兴。

白马：我很高兴。

乌达木：我们都高兴。

白马：高兴就唱首歌吧！

乌达木：唱什么？

白马：唱《奔驰的马》。

乌达木：唱《千里马》。

白马：《奔驰的马》。

乌达木：《千里马》。

白马：让石头、剪刀、布来决定。

乌达木：剪刀！

白马：石头！我赢了。你唱《奔驰的马》。

乌达木：你听到我说剪刀了。

白马：没听到你说剪刀，我怎么选择呢？先听后选。

乌达木：算你赢了。我唱《奔驰的马》。

乌达木唱：

作词：格·巴图呼

作曲：楚伦巴图

汉语填词：布仁巴雅尔

它吻土撒野时高山会低头

它抢缰前冲时大地会颤动

它旋转身躯时太阳会跟随

骑着它，晨起赶早奔跑时衣袍会泄暖

陶林骏马的飞尘，使人斗志昂扬

冠军奖牌叫名时，使人泪流满面

陶林骏马的奔跑中彩旗在飘扬

这就是蒙古那达慕

它咬紧嚼子嘶鸣时栓子也会心跳
它收缰稳衡漫步时拧绳会反弹
它路过他乡营地时吸引羡慕的眼球
让它静心小歇时风才会歇脚

仙鹤色的骏马被赞美奶酒会已抢光
银饰鞍上的主人一瞬间变得很威风
仙鹤色的骏马旋风中彩旗在飘扬
这是蒙古那达慕

深夜谷粮传说在开话匣老人在讲述
清晨骑手之歌一唱响帐房空荡荡
半午骑手匆忙一处跑跟随如洪流
陶林骏马在领先哈达会断缺

健壮骏马的汗水湿透了那达慕的赛场
外哈拉哈的家乡里无与伦比的那达慕

健壮骏马在奔跑中歌声飘扬

这是蒙古那达慕

白马：我喜欢你唱歌的模样，尤其是你唱《奔驰的马》。那边也有人在唱歌，我们去看看。

乌达木：去听听。

白马：他“唱得好看”!

乌达木：别取笑我了。我小时候说“老师说我唱得好看”是因为我当时国语说得不够好。现在 perfect。

白马：什么是 perfect?

乌达木：亲爱的马，我觉得你很啰嗦。你听

得出那个叔叔在唱什么吗？

白马：我知道是你专辑里的一首歌，但不记得歌名了。

乌达木：《巴特尔舅舅》。

白马：对，对，《巴特尔舅舅》。加入他们，一起唱吧。

乌达木：不要打扰他和孩子们。

白马：那边有很多姑娘载歌载舞，她们唱的是长调，对吧？

乌达木：是。

白马：加入她们吧！

乌达木：好主意！

乌达木从两个女生之间的裙逢中钻进了姑娘们围成的那个圈圈中间。

乌达木成了花心，在中间跳着舞。

姑娘们开始没有看清新来的花心是乌达木。等看清楚了是谁，突然停住了唱歌，一起喊：乌达木做我的男朋友吧！我是你的粉丝“牧草”。

白马大喊：木木快上马。

乌达木又从两个姑娘的裙逢中钻了出来，飞身上马。

白马驮着木木奔驰远去。

姑娘们也都不甘落后，骑上马追赶，并喊着“乌达木——”“乌达木——”

白马：终于甩掉了她们。否则，你今天可能会被选去当某人家的女婿了。

乌达木：当女婿？我还不够年龄。要不是你在那里喊，我还真想同那群美丽的姑娘们再多跳一会儿。

白马：我们时间不多了。那边还有射箭比赛。

乌达木：我们时间不多了。

白马：我们时间是不多了！

乌达木：时间不多就不去射箭了。

白马：看样子，你对射箭没有兴趣。

乌达木：我想家了。

白马：那我们回家吧。

乌达木调转马头。

白马：回家的路途很遥远，唱首歌吧！唱你想唱的《千里马》吧。

乌达木唱《千里马》：

蒙古民歌
汉语填词：布仁巴雅尔

塔力雅图和麦丹两地间
没想到路途这么遥远
要知道有这么遥远

换着骑那健壮的千里马有多好

哈日干图和麦丹两地间
没想到路途这么遥远
要知道有这么遥远
换着骑那白额头的千里马有多好

霍鲁斯图和麦丹两地间
没想到路途这么遥远
要知道有这么遥远
换着骑那飞快的千里马有多好

麦丹和哈日干图两地间
没想到路途这么遥远
要知道有这么遥远
换着骑那白额头的千里马有多好

白马：我正是你要的千里马。

乌达木：我知道你是我的千里马。

白马：你怎么知道？

乌达木：这是秘密。

白马：我想喝水。

乌达木：清晨你不是喝过水了吗？

白马：别忘了，我不是骆驼。骆驼喝一下，管很久。我喝一下，只管一下。

乌达木：你的一下是多久？

白马：一下就是一下。

乌达木：我们有类沟，我跟你说不清。总之，我知道你又渴了，又需要喝水了。我们现在离 18 弯河很远了，离额尔古纳河近一些，我带你去。

白马：其实，对草原我比你更熟悉。清晨天黑又有雾，我看不清楚。现在是白天，我带你去。

乌达木：你知道哪条河是额尔古纳河?

白马：我们现在离边境很近了，顺着走，就能到达。

过了半个时辰。

白马：我看见额尔古纳河了。

乌达木：我也看见了。

白马：瞧，对面是俄国的一个村庄。

乌达木：我在想，古时，没有铁丝网，两国边境的村民是如何相处的？

白马：不要去想过去了。我去喝水，你也喝点水吧。我知道你平时都喝自来水或瓶装水。今天，你也只有河水喝了。希望人类不要污染河水，因为他们也会有喝河水的时候。

乌达木：我会向人民政府转达你的希望。

白马：希望人民政府会像你这样有反应。

乌达木：我会向人民政府转达你的希望。

白马：你好像归心似箭，心不在焉的样子。同样的一句话说两遍。

乌达木：我是认真的。

乌达木和白马在返回的路途中，已经走了很久了。

前方出现了一个敖包。

乌达木：请在前面的敖包处停下来。

白马：你出来的时候不是拜过了吗？怎么又要拜一下？

乌达木：你知道吗？

白马：你不说，我怎么知道？

乌达木：我想说，干爸和干妈本可以不管我，可他们用人间最真诚的爱把我变成了他们的责任，他们为我做了一切他们能做的事情，他们同我一起悲伤，他们同我一起欢乐，他们资助我读书，他们给我最好的音乐教育，他们陪我成长。我在他们的生活中，他们在我的生活里。并且是永远，永远，永远……

白马：我好羡慕你。

乌达木：你有理由羡慕我。我现在真的好幸福。有天堂里的阿爸和额吉的祝福，有干爸和干妈在现实生活中的看护和教导，我还需要什么？

白马：你干爸不是说，他不想做你的好

人吗？

乌达木：他的意思是说他不想夺爱。

白马：我不明白。

乌达木：换句话说，干爸认为我是我阿爸额吉的宝贝，他只想替我的阿爸额吉看护这个宝贝，而无意拥有这个宝贝。实际上干爸和干妈和我自己的阿爸和额吉在我的心里有着同样的位置。我即爱自己的阿爸额吉，也爱我的干爸干妈。他们都是像蜡烛一样燃烧自己，照亮我。

白马：他们希望你长大后能照亮更多的人。

乌达木：我会的。不过干爸和干妈这样的称呼不同于蒙语文化，喊起来有些怪怪的。

白马：文化是可以借用的，只要是好的文化，都可以用心去接受。干是指没有血缘关系，但重要的部分是妈和爸这两个字。你这样急着回家，我猜想你一定是想你的干爸干妈了吧？

乌达木：是的，现在我即想念我的阿爸和额吉，也想念干爸和干妈。

乌达木和白马到达了敖包处。

乌达木下马，朝敖包跪下。

乌达木：蒙语中的称呼阿爸和额吉将永远留给天上的阿爸和额吉。请阿爸和额吉让我使用国语中的爸爸和妈妈来称呼我的干爸和干妈吧！因为他们在替你们照顾我。

乌达木起身。

乌达木：亲爱的马，可以快点回家吗？我想把自己的心愿告诉我的干爸和干妈。

白马：快是没有问题的。我不仅是千里马，我还是一匹会飞的马。不过时辰还未到。如果我是你，会先在这里练习一下喊妈妈和爸爸。

乌达木：问题是，你不是我。我等不及了，能快点带我回家吗？要喊也不是在这里喊。

白马：虽然时辰未到，我们不等了。你是草原小王子，你说了算。

白马蹲下，乌达木上马。

白马“嗖”的一声，飞了起来。

一眨眼到家了。

乌达木看到自己已经站在家的门前，上前用力地敲门。

白马：你不会按门铃吗？

乌达木：来不及了！

白马：家里好像没有人。

乌达木大声喊："爸爸"、"妈妈"

乌达木的干爸和干妈听到喊声，从厨房跑进乌达木的卧室。

问：儿子，儿子，你怎么了？你没事吧？

乌达木从梦中醒过来，看到干爸和干妈。

问：我到家了吗？

干妈：是，你在家，孩子。怎么了？为什么说你到家了吗？出什么事了吗？

乌达木：没有，我很好。我只是做了一个奇怪的梦。我和我的马，还有——

乌达木从床上跳了下来。

说：干爸干妈，我又梦到我的阿爸和额吉了，我好想念我的阿爸和额吉。每当想到他们，我的心好痛，好痛！不能自已。

干爸搂住乌达木。

干爸说：我们理解。

乌达木：谢谢干爸和干妈的理解。但是当我远离你们的时候，我也非常想念你们。请允许我把蒙语中的称呼阿爸和额吉永远留给我梦中的阿爸和额吉，请允许我用国语中的爸爸妈妈来称呼你们。这么多年来，你们一直在陪我悲伤，陪我欢乐。尤其是在我还没有进入星空之前，在我还没有“牧草”的日子里，是你们没有放弃我，是你们一直在关注我，资助我，教导我，陪我一起成长。你们爱我，指导我，培育我就如同爸爸和妈妈。我爱你们就像爱我自己的阿爸和额吉。

干爸和干妈：你是上帝送给我们的儿子，你给我们的生活带来了无比的快乐。我们很荣幸能够“接力”做你的爸爸和妈妈。我们愿同你一起悲伤，和你一起欢乐。你愿意做我们的儿子吗？

乌达木：我愿意。

爸爸和妈妈拥抱着乌达木。说：我们是吉祥的一家。

乌达木：我们是吉祥的一家：爸爸和妈妈，

奶奶和叔叔，还有3个姐姐。诺尔曼是我的大姐，苏尼尔是我的二姐，英格玛是我的三姐。

白马走了进来。说："还有我。还有我。"

大家说："对，还有你，Dear Horse。我们是吉祥如意的一家。"

众人一起唱《吉祥三宝》。

《吉祥三宝》

作词作曲：布仁巴雅尔

阿爸，太阳出来月亮回家了吗？

对啦！

星星出来太阳去哪里了？

在天上！

我怎么找也找不到它？

它回家了！

太阳月亮星星就是吉祥的一家！

阿妈，叶子绿了什么时候开花？

等夏天来了！

花儿红了果实能去摘吗？

等秋天到啦！

果实种在土里能发芽吗?

她会长大的!

花儿叶子果实就是吉祥的一家!

宝贝，爸爸像太阳照着妈妈!

那妈妈呢?

妈妈像绿叶托着红花!

我呢?

你像种子一样正在发芽!

我们就是吉祥如意的一家！

（完）

At Mid—night, Uudam is having a dream.

In his dream, Uudam, in pajamas, gets lost on a foggy immense grassland in Inner Mongolia, China. He cannot see anything around. He has no idea where he is.

"Uudam, Uudam!" Undam hears a voice calling his name. Uudam turns around and sees a handsome white horse walking towards him. Uudam looks at the white horse with amazement. The white horse gets down and Uudam gets on the horse.

Uudam: Where are we? Where are you going to take me?

White Horse: Do you have GPS?

Uudam: No, I do not have my GPS with me.

White Horse: Well, we can use the Big Dipper for directions. Let's stroll around. As long as we make it back before midnight the same day next year, I can take you home in time.

Uudam: What did you mean?

White Horse: I feel lonely. Could you please forget about your school and accompany me for a while?

Uudam: All right, for you only.

They see an AoBao ahead.

Uudam: Please stop at the first AoBao we see.

White Horse: We don't have much time. Don't be long.

At the AoBao, Uudam gets off his white horse and gets down on his knees.

Uudam: If there is really Heaven up there, I hope aaβ and eej met in Heaven and kept each other company. Dear Aaβ and Eej, your son Uudam wishes so much he could live in this world with you guys forever. Your son Uudam misses you guys so much.

Uudam gets up and cirlces around the AoBao three times counter clock wise. Then he climbs on the white horse. They move on.

A while of silence.

White Horse: Would you like to go back to those days?

Uudam: Yes, if I could.

White Horse: But as you know, time won't go back. There is really no time tunnel for which humans have always wished.

Uudam: But there is time tunnel on my mind. I could fly back to those days on my mind.

White Horse: In reality, time is traveling forward. Everything has to move forward. It is God's will.

Uudam: God bless everybody.

White Horse: I am thirsty. When can I have water to drink?

Uudam: When you see a river , you have water.

White Horse: I agree with you. Where there is a river, there is water. But where is the river?

Udam: I am thirsty, too. There are seven rivers running across Hulunbuir Grassland. Just be patient, my friend.

Udam: There is a river on the grassland, which we call Morgle River. Morgle River is known as the most winding river in China. Along the border with Russia is Argun River. The names of the other rivers are ...

White Horse: You are trying to make me feel better by talking about rivers and talking about water in the rivers. But talked water is talked water. Real water is real water.

Udam: I hope you keep your hope up.

The night is dark.

Uudam: Listen, there is water running. That's Morgle River, I bet you.

White Horse: It is so dark that I cannot see anything. I don't see any river running around.

Uudam: It won't escape my ears. Keep to the left, buddy.

White Horse: Where is the river, then?

Uudam: Just a little longer, buddy. It is right ahead.

White Horse: Oh water! I see it now. There it is. My hope comes true!

Uudam: You drink water. I will make a bonfire for us.

The bonfire lights up both the river and the grassland and it lights up both Uudam's face and the face of the white horse. Uudam is lying on the grassland by the bonfire, looking up into the sky.

White Horse: Why don't you go and take a drink? What are you thinking about?

Uudam: I am thinking of my aaβ and my eej. They gave me life and looked after me. Aaβ and Eej's job was to watch and herd the sheep of others. They were happy sheepherders. After a day's work, they came home together. When I was still very little, they left me and went to Heaven hand in hand. They now rest in peace in Heaven. They were great parents to me. I am very proud of them. I miss them. I miss the time my mother and I spent together singing. I miss the days my father and I spent together doing horseback riding and galloping across the grassland. They will live on and on in my heart forever and ever.

White Horse: I don't have aaβ and eej, either. I look forward and go on with my life. I am becoming stronger in every way every day. Though it is true that you keep me company, don't you think it is also the fact that I keep you company? Now my job is to stay with you and keep you company. With humans around, you need to act like a real man. In our Mongolian culture, a man's tears are pearls. A man needs to hold back his tears. But being with me, you do not have to be a man.

Udam: So what am I supposed to be?

White Horse: Yourself.

Uudam: I feel like singing a song now.

White Horse: Go ahead.

Uudam is singing:

Flowers wish to be in the soil rather than to
Be picked.
My eej always held my hand in hers,
Softly telling me their wishes.

Far away eej you are,
But you are still holding my hand
In my dream.

Sometimes my eyes are covered
By the sandy winds.
But I wish I could always hear
My eej calling me.
Where are you, my eej?
How I wish you could kiss me again!
Far away my eej you are,
You are still kissing me in my dream.

At this point, Uudam could not help crying hard, weeping hard and sobbing hard. Tears are all over his face. He then continues his singing:

You want me to be as brave as an eagle

That flies through the clouds.
You want me to be as strong as the flowers
That wave in the wind.
When I go on to stride forward,
I know you are always there with me.
Far away my eej you are,
You are still hugging me
In your arms in my dream.

White Horse: That song is *Eej In The Dream*.

Uudam: How do you know?

White Horse: Everybody knows it. Every horse knows it. The whole country knows that you miss your eej all day long.

Uudam: I miss my eej every minute and second. My eej taught me many songs. *Eej In The Dream* is one of them. I sing this song to remember her.

White Horse: You cried, wept and sobbed like a woman. Do you feel better?

Uudam: Yes, I do.

White Horse: I know you miss your aaβ, too.

Uudam: Yes, I do. In those days when my aaβ was tending sheep, I went to help. One day I was doing my homework, a little lam swallowed my paper.

White Horse: Is that so?

Undam: Yes, it is true.

White Horse: Do you know how to mimic the sound sheep make?

Uudam: Of course, I can do it.

White Horse: Then do it.

Uudam: Baa Baa Baa

Uudam: You don't know I can make your voice, do you?

White Horse: Then do it.

Uudam: Listen up.

White Horse: I am listening.

Uudam: Listen up.

White Horse: I am listening. Go ahead, please.

Uudam: Neigh Neigh Neigh

White Horse: Wow, a wonderful job! That's exactly what I do. I suspect you were a horse in your previous life.

Uudam: Why don't you say that I were a sheep?

White Horse: All right, you were a sheep and I were a human.

Uudam: Why don't you say you were a sheep?

White Horse: All right, I were a sheep and you were not a human.

Uudam: Be nice, man.

White Horse: Once in a while, I'd like to have some sense of humor. In fact, I am not a good speechmaker. Actually when I say you are not a human, I meant to say you are an eagle that flies across our inner Mongolian sky. Actually what I really meant to say is you are a great kid. You are a Baateer to your grandmother. You are also a Baateer in my heart. All right, since you miss your aaβ, too, sing a song *Dedicated To Father*.

Uudam is singing *Dedicated To Father*:

The autumn wind is blowing .
The grass turns yellow.
Getting old is my father.
At the time deer are big and strong,
I will go back hometown.
I wish I could see my father
Before the river runs freezing.

Hills and mountains are seen
In the distance.
I miss my father.
The river water is crystal—clear
As my aaβ's kind heart.

At the time deer are big and strong,
I will go back hometown.
I wish I could see my father
Before the river runs freezing.

Autumn is coming.
Getting old is my father.
I cannot wait to see my father.
My father will be happy to see me
With tears in his eyes.
At the time deer are big and strong,
I will go back hometown.
I wish I could see my father
Before the river runs freezing.

White Horse: Your singing was full of deep feelings and very touching. It makes me begin to think of my own father and mother.

Uudam: My parents were the first stage rocket that carried me into the space close to stars. My godparents are the second stage rocket that sent me over to the space where stars are shinning. I became a new star. I am now a twinkling little star. But at a huge cost. My father and mother dedicated their lives to my achievement and my godfather and godmother have dedicated their love and their full support to my success.

White Horse: That's God's will. You were born to be a good singer. You are one of the prides of our Inner Mongolia.

After a while.

White Horse: What do you want to be when you grow up?

Udam: I want to be a scientist.

White Horse: Don't forget that you were a born singer. You don't want to give up on singing, do you?

Udam: Would you believe if a Mongolian tells you that he would quit singing?

White Horse: I am talking about being a professional.

Udam: My godfather is a journalist. He works at China Radio International (CRI). He performs singing as well. I can be a singer as well as a scientist as long as my singing is beloved.

White Horse: I can picture the green magic ink you invented in your songs. I can smell the fragrance of the green grass in your songs. I can hear rivers running in your songs. I also can hear thousand— mile horses galloping in your songs. Your songs are filled with your deep feelings for your late parents. Very very touching and moving. Your songs make the listeners rethink about their relationship with their parents and make the listeners rethink about the way they treat the nature. I am a big fan of yours.

Uudam: Thank you, dear fan. Let's go if you are done taking a drink.

White Horse: Yes, Sir, my grassland prince.

Uudam: Let's run to see who runs faster. You know that I am a gold medal winner in tracks at school, don't you? I beat everyone in men's 1 000—meter event at my school.

White Horse: Let's do it. You will see who is the loser.

Uudam and his horse start off, run, run and run. Uudam is far behind. The white horse turns around to see Uudam left far behind. The white horse comes back and gets down. Uudam climbs on.

White Horse: Have you found that humans

have limitations?

Uudam: I never said we humans don't have limitations. Could you keep quiet about it?

White Horse: No problem to keep quiet. Listen, all I intend to say is that both mankind and animalkind have both strong points and weak points. All I intend to say is that mutual respect is significant. All I intend to say is that you and I could learn from each other. All I intend to say is that it is good to keep good relationship with each other.

Uudam: Did you ever read books?

White Horse: This is common sense. Many books were written based on common sense. No common sense, no books !

White Horse: Good morning. It is morning time. The fog is gone. Look! Look! A big crowd is over there. What are those people doing there? Look, someone is using a torch to start a flame in the center ground.

Uudam: It must be Naadam.

White Horse: What is Naadam ?

Uudam: Naadam is a once—a—year event, a traditional festival for Mongolians.

White Horse: Who is the guy that is lighting the flame?

Uudam: A baateer.

White Horse: What is baateer?

Uudam: Baateer is hero. A person with integrity and morals and did many good things. Only just now, you said I am your baateer.

White Horse: Did I?

Uudam: Didn't you?

White Horse: Of course, I said it.

Uudam: Of course, you said it.

White Horse: What are they singing?

Uudam: If you listen carefully, you will grasp those words.

On the green grassland, the big crowd at the festival party is singing:

See the lucky white clouds
Hanging high up in the blue sky
See the colorful flowers
In full bloom on the grassland

Harvest season gathers Genghis Khan's
Children together for Naadam

The riders are riding their horses
Galloping across the grassland

The girls are shooting arrows
With their crescent — moon— like bows

Seniors are presenting Khadags to Baateers
An old aaB is offering his wine to
The God of Bravery
Ah ha ha

Many heroes in this area
They are Mongolians on this grassland

Night falls
Millions of stars twinkling in the sky
Warm bonfires everywhere

Folks from all directions are having fun
At Naadam

Raise your glasses of wine to each other
Sing *Beautiful Grassland Is My Home*
Listen to the Morin Quur and enjoy
Its beautiful melody of *Thousands of*
Horses Galloping Across The Grassland

Ah ha ha

Come on, let's dance arm in arm
Come on, let's sing heart to heart
And heart to heart we are singing

White Horse: Horse racing must be part of Naadam. Am I right? Would you like to take part in the race?

Uudam: Would you like to take part in the race?

White Horse: Would you?

Uudam: Dear White Horse, don't talk too much. Let's just go ahead to compete with those racers. Go, get into the tracks.

White Horse flies over the crowd and lands right on the start line. Upon hearing the sound of the starter pistol, Uudam and his horse make a good start, now they are among the racers, before long, they get ahead of others. The spectators recognize Uudam and begin to chant Uudam Uudam, go Uudam, go Uudam, Uudam . Uudam and his white horse cross the finish line first. They win.

Uudam: Victory! Thank you Thank you,

my dear white horse.

White Horse: When did you become so polite?

Uudam: It is something from my heart. We've got to run now, or we won't be able to get out of here when my fans all come to me for my autograph.

White Horse: What is that pile doing?

Uudam: Can you use the word "crowd" instead of "pile"?

White Horse: Oh, excuse me. No offense.

Uudam: You are excused.

White Horse: You haven't answered my question yet.

Uudam: What question?

White Horse: What is that pile doing? I am sorry about the wrong word. What is that CROWD doing? I mean those who are wearing colorful flags around their necks.

Uudam: Those who are wearing colorful flags around their necks are wrestlers.

White Horse: Are you planning to take part in wrestling competition?

Uudam: Are you ?

White Horse: Anything to do with me?

Uudam: Just give it a try.

White Horse: You should be the one who gives it a try. Not me.

Uudam: I will.

White Horse: I can help you with horse racing. When it comes to wrestling, the only thing I can do is stand back and watch.

Uudam: Then you stand back and watch.

Uudam makes a few backwards steps and then jumps high over the crowd and into the field. The match starts. Uudam and his opponent are taking off form each side, dancing forward like eagle's flying, to meet each other. When the two meet in the middle, they shake hands and solute each other. Before long, the audience sees Uudam being lifted and toppled to the ground. The bout is finished. Uudam's opponent helps undam get back on his feet. Uudam's opponent is declared the winner. According to the rule, the winner stays for the next bout and the loser leaves. Uudam shakes hands with the winner and leaves the field.

Uudam and his white horse then continue their fun searching.

White Horse: Since you knew you would not be able to beat him, why did you do it?

Uudam: For Chandmani Erdene.

White Horse: You mean for you, for your godfather and for your godmother.

Uudam: For another three valuable reasons. If you lose, it may mean you are physically not strong enough to compete and you need to improve your strength. Aside from that, you need to have a strong willpower and have a good sportsmanship for the competition. That is to say that even if you don't believe you can win, you should try your best, just do it. When you lose, you shake hands with the winner and solute him instead of getting upset or jealous. It is all about strength, willpower and good sportsmanship. That's the three values, in other words, that's the three treasures I am talking about. You have shown them to me. You have the same three values as I do.

White Horse: You think so?

Uudam: Not only do I think so, I also saw the 3 values in you and in your buddies. I learned a lot from you guys.

White Horse: It is nice of you to say so. You made my day.

Uudam: You made my day too.

White Horse: I am happy.

Uudam: I am happy too.

White Horse: Since you are happy, sing a song for me.

Uudam: What song would you like me to sing?

White Horse: *Galloping Horse*

Uudam: *Thousand—Mile Horse*

White Horse: *Galloping Horse*

Uudam: *Thousand—Mile Horse*

White Horse: Let "Rock, Scissors and Paper" decide which song you should sing.

Uudam: "Scissors".

White Horse: "Rock". I won. You sing *Galloping Horse*.

Uudam: You heard me say "scissors".

White Horse: That's why I chose "Rock". Hear first, then choose.

Uudam: All right, you won. I will sing *Galloping Horse*.

Uudam is singing:

The mountains bow
When she kisses the ground
The earth quakes when she is galloping

Across the grassland
The sun follows when she turns her body
Around and around
Riding her, though feeling chilly
As the wind blows the robe open at down

The riders get hyped up
With handsome Taolin horses galloping by
And kicking up dust behind them
Tears are running down their faces
When the winners are granted the medals
Handsome Taolin horses galloping across
And colorful flags waving in the sky

That is Naadam

While she neighs as she bites the bit tightly
The typing post feels her heartbeat

As the bridle relaxes
While she is taking a slow walk
The lead rope bounces back and forth
She catches all eyes
When she is passing by some camps
The wind stands still when she is relaxing

White horses are praised
Milk and wine are finished fast
The riders are feeling so proud
In the silver—piece—decorated saddles
Handsome white horses galloping across
And colorful flags waving in the sky

That is Naadam

Late night, elders are telling

Wonderful old stories to the young
Early morning, when the riders begin to
Sing *The Song Of The Riders*
The tents are left empty
At mid noon, all the riders are gathering
And racing hard like ocean waves
Handsome Taolin horses are leading
Khadags are running out

Strong horses are sweating
Their sweat is wetting the Naadam ground

Naadam Naadam
Fabulous Naadam
Gorgeous Naadam

Strong horses are running around
Folks from all directions are singing merrily

That is Naadam

White Horse: I enjoy your performance, esp. the way and the style you sing *Galloping Horse*. Buddy, someone else is singing. Let's take a look.

Uudam: Let's take a listen.

White Horse: His singing "looks" great.

Uudam: Quit teasing me again. When I was very little and my mandarin was not very good, I said that my teacher said my singing "looks" good. Actually you know I meant to say my teacher said my singing "sounds" good. Now my mandarin is perfect.

White Horse: What does "perfect" mean?

Uudam: Dear horse, you talk too much. Can you tell what song the man is singing?

White Horse: If my memory is correct, it is one of the songs in your CD album.

Uudam: You have a good memory! It is one of the songs in my album. It is *Uncle Baateer*.

White Horse: *Uncle Baateer*, *Uncle Baateer*. That's the Song title I was about to tell you. Join him so you guys sing together.

Uudam: Don't disturb him and the kids,

they are really having fun.

White Horse: Look! There are many girls dancing and singing over there. They are singing Urtyn Duu if I am right.

Uudam: You are absolutely right. They are singing Urtyn Duu.

White Horse: Join them.

Uudam: Not a bad idea !

Uudam slips into the circle through the narrow gap between the Mongolian robes of two girls. Uudam is now the center of the circle. He is dancing wildly with those beautiful girls. All of a sudden, the girls recognize who he is. They all quit singing and dancing, and begin shouting "Uudam" "Uudam"... "Will you be my boyfriend? I am your fan."

White Horse shouts: Uudam Uudam, come on, let's go.

Uudam slips out of the circle through a narrow gap of two robes, and jumps on his horse. His white horse is carrying him and galloping away. Meanwhile, the girls are going wild and all swiftly get on their own horses and begin chasing Uudam and screaming "Uudam" "Uudam"...

White Horse: Finally we got rid of them. Otherwise, you might have become son-in-law of one girl's parents.

Uudam: I am too young to be son—in—law of a girl's parents. That is not going to happen recently. If not for you, I could dance more with those gorgeous girls.

White Horse: We don't have much time for more fun at one spot. Archery competition is right over there.

Uudam: We don't have much time.

White Horse: Indeed we don't have much time!

Uudam: Since we don't have much time, I don't think we should go shooting arrows.

White Horse: You don't seem to be interested in archery, I can tell.

Udam: I am homesick now.

White Horse: O. K, let's go home right now.

White Horse and Uudam turn around heading home.

White Horse: It is going to be a long way before we get home. Can you sing another song for me? Now you can sing *Thousand — Mile Horse* if you like.

Uudam is singing :

T town and M town are far apart
If I had known the distance
Between T and M is this far
I'd have switched to that strong
And powerful thousand—mile horse

R town and M town are far apart
If I had known the distance
Between R and M is this far
I 'd have switched to thousand—mile horse
The one with white forehead

H town and M town are far apart
If I had known the distance
Between H and M is this far
I 'd have switched to that strong
And fast thousand—mile horse

M town and R town are far apart
If I had known the distance
Between M and R is this far
I'd have switched to thousand—mile horse
The one with white forehead

White Horse: Actually I am your thousand — mile horse. I have both speed and stamina.

Uudam: I know you are and I know you do.

White Horse: How did you know?

Uudam: It's a secret.

White Horse: Can I have some water to drink?

Uudam: You drank water early this morning. Why do you need to drink again?

White Horse: I did drink water early this morning. But don't forget I am not a camel. A camel drinks once for good. I drink once just for once.

Uudam: How long is your once?

White Horse: Once is once.

Uudam: We are of different species. Communication between us is not easy. Anyway, I know you are getting thirsty again. You are dying for water. We have now drifted far away from Morgle River. We are closer to Argun River. I will take you to Argun River.

White Horse: Actually I know this grassland better than you do. It was so dark early in the morning I could not tell for sure where is where. I will be your guide now. Follow me.

Uudam: I have to follow you. I am on your back. You won't get lost, will you?

White Horse: We are close to the border. If we go along the border, we will get to Argun River soon.

One hour later

White Horse: There it is. I see Argun River.

Uudam: So do I.

White Horse: Look, there is a Russian village on the Russian side.

Uudam: I am wondering, in ancient times with no iron wire fence between two countries, how the villagers from both sides got along with one another.

White Horse: Forget about ancient times, would you? I am going to drink some water now. Come on, you too need to drink some water . I know you usually drink bottled water or tap water. Today, you have no choice. I do hope that humans do not pollute river waters. Because somewhere and sometime for some reason humans may have to drink river water as we do.

Uudam: I will pass your hope to the People's Government.

White Horse: I do hope the People's Government will respond to my hope as you do.

Uudam: I will pass your hope to People's Government.

White Horse: I know you are in a hurry to go back home. You didn't seem to pay attention to what I was saying. Because the same line was repeated again and again.

Uudam: I am serious.

It has been a while since Uudam and his horse are on their way back home.

An AoBao appears ahead.

Uudam: Stop by that AoBao, please.

White Horse: You prayed this morning. Why do you need to pray again?

Uudam: Do you know why?

White Horse: If you don't tell me, how do I know why?

Uudam: My godparents could have left me alone, not giving me any of their help because they were not my godparents when my parents died. I was not their responsibility at all. However, they offered their help in every way. They shared both my sadness and happiness. They support me financially so that I can continue to go to school and continue to be able to sing and sing better and better from music education and music training provided by them. They are always around and always there for me as I am growing up. I am in their life and they are in my life forever and ever.

White Horse: I envy you.

Uudam: You have all reasons to envy me. I have a happy life with my aaβ and eej's blessing and with the good care and love of my godparents. I can't expect more than that.

White Horse: I heard your godfather say that he doesn't want to be your good man. Correct me if I am wrong.

Uudam: He meant to say he doesn't want to own the treasure.

White Horse: It doesn't make sense to me.

Uudam: In other words, for example, assuming that I am a dear treasure of my aaβ and eej, my godfather doesn't want to take this treasure away from my aaβ and eej. He just wants to babysit me for my aaβ and eej. However, my godparents have the same spot in my heart as my aaβ and eej do. I love my aaβ and eej dearly and I love my godparents dearly, too. They are all candles that burn themselves to give light to me.

White Horse: They want you to give light to others in the future.

Uudam: I will. Well, the thing is to have godparents is not natural part of our Mongolian custom and culture. When I call my godparents god—dad and god—mom, I feel kind of weird.

White Horse: I understand that to have godparents is not part of Mongolian custom or culture. However, as long as it is something good, accept it with your heart. I understand there is no blood relationship between godkids and godparents. It doesn't mean you guys cannot develop a relationship beyond that. I can tell that you are in a hurry to go back home for you must miss your godparents very much.

Uudam: I guess you are a mind reader. Yes, I miss them very much as well as I miss my aaβ and eej.

In front of the AoBao, Uudam jumps off his white horse and gets down on his knees.

Uudam: I will reserve the Mongolian titles Aaβ and Eej for my late father and late mother.

Dear Aaβ and Eej, I know you can hear me. Please allow me to use Dad and Mom for my god—dad and god—mom for they are looking after me for you guys as parents do.

Uudam gets up.

Uudam: Dear White Horse, can you hurry up? I can't wait to get home. I need to tell my godparents about my decision.

White Horse: No problem to rush home. I am not only a thousand—mile horse, also I am a flying horse. The problem is it is not yet planned time to go home. If I were you, I would practice the new way to call your godparents right here and right now.

Uudam: The matter is that you were not me. I cannot wait to see them and call them Dad and Mom before them.

White Horse: All right, let's not worry about planned time. You are the prince on this grassland. You are the boss. Let's go home now as you wish. May you always get your wishes!

The white horse gets down. Uudam climbs on. The white horse immediately takes off and flies away with Uudam.

Less than a second, Uudam finds himself standing right in front of the door of his godparents' house. Uudam knocks hard at the door.

White Horse: Don't you know how to press the doorbell?

Uudam: No time to do it.

White Horse: Seems as though nobody is in.

Uudam shouts loudly : Mom ! Dad!

Uudam's godparents heard Uudam calling them. They ran from Kitchen to Uudam's bedroom, asking, "What's up, son? Are you okay?"

Uudam wakes up from his dream, looking at his godparents and asking: "Have I arrived home yet?"

God-mom: Of course, you are at home. What has happened? Why did you ask if you have arrived home?

Uudam: I am fine. I just had a very strange dream. In my fairy-tale dream, my horse and me ...

Uudam jumps out of his bed and says: God—dad, God—mom , I believe that I saw my aaB and eej again in my dream. As you know, every time I am thinking of them, my heart is full of pains. So much I wish I could have a chance to see them again in the real world. I miss them so much.

Godfather hugs Uudam and says: We understand about your pains. We understand how much you miss your parents. We do understand.

Uudam: So much I appreciate your understanding! However, it is a fact when I am away from home, I also miss you guys a great deal . I will keep the Mongolian titles AaB and Eej for my late parents.

Please allow me to use Dad and Mom instead of God—dad and God—mom for you. All these years, it is you, my godparents who have stayed by me, sharing both my sadness and happiness. It is you, my godparents who didn't leave me alone, loving me, supporting me, guiding me and watching me grow up. As godparents, you have done everything you can for me like any parents do everything they can for their own kids. Thank you, mom and dad for all your love and for the family you gave me. In my heart, you are my parents already.

God—dad and God—mom: Son, you are a gift to us from God. You have brought us a lot of fun. We feel honored to be your dad and mom after all have happened. We shared and we will share your sadness if any. We shared and we will love to share your happiness. You are a member of our family and you are our dear son.

Uudam: You are my dear dad and mom.

Dad and Mom hug Uudam in their arms, saying, "We are one family. We are a lucky family. Thanks to God and thanks to everybody in this family."

Uudam: I am a lucky member of this lucky family. I have mom, dad, grandmother, uncle, and three sisters.

Uudam's white horse walks in and says: "me, me, me too is a lucky member of your lucky family."

Dad and Mom and Uudam all say to White

Horse, "Absolutely, you are a lucky member of our lucky family, Mr. Me."

And all begin to sing the song of *Chandmani Erdene*:

Undam and W. Horse: Dad

Dad: Yes?

Undam and W. Horse: Is the moon home when the sun comes out?

Dad: Right.

Undam and W. Horse: Where is the sun when the stars come out?

Dad: In the sky.

Undam and W. Horse: How come I can't find it?

Dad: It went home.

Chorus: The sun and the moon and the stars are a lucky family.

Undam and W. Horse: Mom

Mom: Yes?

Undam and W. Horse: With leaves green, when will flowers blossom ?

Mom: When the summer is here.

Undam and W. Horse: Can we pick the fruits when the flowers are in full bloom?

Mom: When autumn is here.

Undam and W. Horse: Can fruits spout when they fall into the soil?

Mom: The seeds will grow.

Chorus: Leaves and flowers and the fruits are a lucky family.

Dad and Mom: Dear

Undam and W. Horse: Yes?

Dad and Mom: Dad is like the sun, shinning on mom.

Undam and W. Horse: How about mom then?

Dad and Mom: Mom is like leaves holding up flowers.

Undam and W. Horse: How about me?

Dad and Mom: You are like seeds sprouting.

Undam and W. Horse: Understand.

Chorus: We are one family. We are a lucky and happy family.

THE END

感谢

Acknowledgements

衷心地感谢布仁老师允许该书使用他的歌曲作词和对外来歌曲的填词。

We wish to thank Mr. Buren Bayaer for allowing this book to use his lyrics.

衷心地感谢周申生先生在将中文翻译成英文中所给予的巨大帮助。

We wish to thank Mr. Shen S. Chou for his great help with the translation of this story from Chinese into English.

衷心地感谢 Heather Miller 女士在一些英文

词汇使用方面给予的确认。

We also wish to thank Mrs. Heather Miller for her great help with some wordings.

张慧 and Feixer Miller

关于作者

About the Authors

张慧，于 1982 年毕业于师范大学。毕业后在一所大专教书。后又到美国进修，并相夫教子。

The author Ms. Zhang Hui, born in China, graduated from a Normal University in China in 1982. Then she taught at a college. Later, she went to U. S. A. for further study. She is both a good wife and a good mother.

费西儿·米勒，于 1980 年代初毕业于国内一所师范学院，到中学教书，之后进入一家合资企业工作。2008 年之前在该公司的美国分公司工作。

The author Ms. Feixer Miller, born in China, graduated from a Normal College in China. After teaching in high school for 3 years, she worked for a joint venture. Before 2008, she worked for the company's branch in Los Angeles.